What Pec

C000103305

"Lynn Fraser and I have years. It has been a expression, her face, and her whole being has shifted, with the falling away of the debilitating trauma reactions that she describes, and that many will find familiar, using the tools she suggests. Lynn's is a voice you can trust, laying it all out in a simple yet profound approach to changing one's relationship to thought, and seeing how it can both contribute to and exacerbate the experience of trauma.

She has willingly and courageously walked the walk; so now she can convincingly talk the talk. Anyone who has lived through trauma (who has not?) would benefit from her kind and skillful guidance. She has been in the combat zone and come back to report the way out. Let Lynn show you a less constricted way to feel, to see, to be. You can feel the invitation to, and from, an easefulness in her words, coming from an equanimity that she has discovered and unveiled, and that is available to all. Lynn knows whereof she speaks. It is peace she offers, with a smile."

Colette Kelso, TheDeepestPeace.com

"All I can say is, this book works. Lynn writes from the space of deep breaths about her own traumas. The reader comes to view their own traumas from that space. At the same time, Lynn is offering release, resolution, and healing. In other words, you will feel safe with Lynn. If you are ready to face the deeply held and constantly emerging sensations and feelings associated with painful memories and thoughts, by all means read this book. Just be sure you are ready, because the journey toward healing is a challenge, and like I said, this book works."

Jerry Katz, Nonduality.org

"Friends with Your Mind is a distillation of the wisdom Lynn has gleaned from twenty- five years of meditation, mindfulness and yoga practice and teaching, along with the insights she has gained since she discovered the Living Inquiries, of which she is a Senior Facilitator. Touching on a wide range of topics, including healing from trauma, fear of flying, and body shaming, Lynn describes how even intense feelings and disturbing thought patterns can be unwound when we know how to do so safely. She offers nuggets from her inspiring personal journey, an understanding of how our minds and bodies operate, and guidance and resources on how to work with thoughts and feelings in an effective way. She demonstrates that it is possible for us to finally have compassion and love for ourselves, our bodies and our minds."

Fiona Robertson, author of The Art of Finding Yourself: Live Bravely and Awaken to Your True Nature

"Lynn Fraser is a teacher of teachers. She has drawn from her own healing journey to write a clear and concise "owner's manual" for the Mind. Born out of her own extensive breathing and meditation practices, Lynn explains how to heal yourself from anxiety, trauma and just the everyday experience of believing our stressful thoughts. This book provides easy to follow explanations and instructions."
Dr. Kay Vogt, Licensed Clinical Psychologist

"This book, Making Friends With Your Mind, lives up to its name! With simple, practical suggestions, Lynn takes the reader through the process of how to change our relationship to thoughts, and how we can free ourselves from the tyranny of our thinking. I love that these techniques are so easy to implement. Lynn speaks from experience. Her dedication and compassion in assisting people to free themselves is boundless."
Fiona Murphy, Clinical Social worker, Certified Living Inquiries Facilitator

"After I had my "awakening", I had a deep sense of peace. I felt I had finally figured it all out. But then came uncertainty. My endless runaway thoughts turned into questioning why anything mattered at all. Fortunately, I had Lynn to help guide me and see that all my thoughts about the meaning of life were just new stories my mind was telling.

In her new book, Lynn brings an anchor of clarity to a stormy sea of thoughts that our minds are always trying to churn up. Along with real-life examples of how our minds tend to race out of control, Lynn uses clear and simple techniques to help us finally get out of our heads and into the moment. Her kindness, compassion and desire to help are evident on every page."

Chad Sewich, Kiloby Center for Recovery

Deep into this book by Lynn Fraser, there is a hero's journey of courage and compassion. It is a step by step journey of how to take the mystery out of healing the nervous system. Often based on her own experience, Lynn shares skillful practices and tools toward this journey. She is a master at breaking down the elements needed toward becoming intimate with how our thinking and nervous system works and making positive change, replacing confusion with confidence. This book offers the strategies required to notice and inquire into the process of thought, how thought has become misinterpreted as who we are, and the courage to explore being with a sensation or feeling rather than merely thinking about it. She points the reader to this healing journey, and the process that brings you to true healing ... making friends with your mind! It is my pleasure to endorse this book. I loved it!

Sutra Ray Robinson, WakeUpSessions.com

Friends With Your Mind

How To Stop Torturing Yourself With Your Thoughts

Lynn Fraser

Stillpoint Publishing

Table of Contents

Foreword

What can I say about Lynn Fraser and her work that you won't discover for yourself in this book? She is a Senior Facilitator of the Living Inquiries, a methodology that I and my other Senior Facilitators created back in 2008 and have continuously developed and refined since then. Lynn has been an integral part of that development all along the way.

She is extremely skillful as a facilitator, and has a special set of skills for working with the mind and body around trauma and addiction. However, she understands how the mind and body work from the perspective of interior awareness regarding a whole host of conditions that one might experience including stress, anxiety, OCD and other obsessions, gender/sexual orientation and relationship issues, depression – the list goes on.

Although Lynn has advanced skills as a teacher, facilitator, meditation leader and trauma specialist, she knows how to simplify this kind of work so that it is accessible to anyone and everyone. She is a teacher in her own right, apart from the work she does with the Living Inquiries. Her skill set is so wide and varied that she can't be pinned down with any labels.

She has experienced a profound recognition of present moment awareness and embodies it naturally. That's the kind of teacher anyone would want, for if one's teacher does not have the direct experience of what is being taught, true transformation just cannot happen.

Lynn is so valuable to me as a Senior Facilitator. When I have someone who needs work with trauma or some other issue but who cannot attend my Kiloby Center for Recovery in Palm Springs, Lynn is one of the first facilitators I consider referring the person to. I know that whomever I refer to Lynn, the person is in great hands. And you are in great hands now that you have this book in your own hands.

This book encapsulates Lynn's ability to break down how suffering happens within our awareness. This is the kind of book that I truly love – one that is very simple and direct with easy to understand instructions that one can translate into his or her own experience almost immediately. I wish this book had been around when I first started being interested in mindfulness. It would have helped me along so much more quickly than other books that I used to read at that time.

We need more books like this, that truly break everything down in a simple way. You won't find a lot of intellectualized pontificating here or complex theories. That's because those kinds of things are not needed to learn to relate differently to our thoughts, emotions and sensations and dissolve our suffering. What is needed is concise, direct instruction and this book is full of that.

Lynn co-leads the Family Services Program at the Kiloby Center for Recovery. She has such a beautiful and peaceful soul. Working with her is a true delight. The families that work with her through my center are always grateful for her wisdom and guidance. I've sent the person who I love the most – my partner – to Lynn for sessions and it has helped him tremendously. He would be proud to give this endorsement himself.

What I invite you to do is take your time and really notice how Lynn is breaking down experience into its simplest parts and then really look into your experience to verify that she has given you a map to suffering and how to heal it.

I leave you in Lynn's more than capable hands. Be good to yourself and sit with this book for some time, really soaking in what it has to say. I know you will be pleased with it! Lynn is being a bit modest with the subtitle. This book can do more than help you stop torturing yourself with thoughts. It can help you come to accept and love your entire experience.

Scott Kiloby, Founder of the Living Inquiries and CEO of the Kiloby Center for Recovery, December 2016

Acknowledgments

I am truly blessed with authentic, generous teachers and friends.

Becoming friends with my mind began through the Himalayan Tradition of Yoga Meditation and my main teachers Swami Veda Bharati and Pandit Hari Shankar Dabral. For twenty-five years, I have been learning and meditating within this tradition. I began to understand myself and heal my mind through this connection and their comprehensive, holistic knowledge.

I met Scott Kiloby in 2008 and trained to be a Facilitator of the Living Inquiries a few years later. I brought the learning and depth of my years of meditation to these simple, profound inquiry practices. I am grateful for Scott's commitment to deep personal inquiry and his generosity in sharing. Through my weekly sessions with Senior Facilitator Colette Kelso and two intensive weeks working with

Scott, early life trauma has healed and I am free to enjoy my life.

I would like to acknowledge and thank my son, Dustin LindenSmith. I admire him so much for his courage, intelligence, and the heartfelt attention and love he brings to family and friends. I so value our close connection.

We are building a lovely community of people who are working with the healing practices of the Living Inquiries and the Himalayan Tradition of Yoga Meditation. Together we are creating safe spaces to be authentic and honest. Thank you to all of you who come to Natural Rest groups and our daily online practices, for showing up and taking the risk to engage. We grow and heal together.

Lane Ledoux is an integral part of my work. She is courageous, smart, persistent, and fully committed to helping bring this healing work out into the world. I am inspired by the deep changes and healing I see in her life and grateful for her support. It is thanks to Lane that I am able to reach out and connect with so many people.

Thank you so much to Scott, Colette, Fiona R, Jerry, Fiona M, Kay, Chad, and Sutra Ray for taking the time to read the manuscript and offer your feedback and endorsements.

Several people read and gave suggestions on the manuscript, including Sheila Rodgers, Lane Ledoux and Dustin LindenSmith. Thank you for your time, attention and honesty. This book is more thorough and complete because of your valuable feedback.

Thank you to everyone who is working to heal. I am inspired every day by your courage and commitment in the face of tremendous struggle and pain. It is possible to heal. I know that to be true for myself and for you.

Introduction

Welcome!

You opened this book because your thoughts are torturing you and you want to end your suffering.

I know about that! Twenty-five years ago my shoulders were like cement from chronic stress. I was shut down emotionally. My thinking was compulsive as I tried in vain to control outer circumstances and people so I could feel better. My life is so different now.

The Living Inquiries and Natural Rest, combined with twenty years of teaching meditation and yoga psychology, are the foundation of my healing work and this book.

The Living Inquiries are a form of mindfulness self-inquiry with which we look at how our thoughts and feelings are Velcroed together creating identification, fear or compulsion. Natural Rest is an ongoing invitation to relax and notice there is a simple, restful awareness here in every moment.

I know about the mind and nervous system. I first learned about the role of the vagus nerve as part of my training in yoga and meditation. When we breathe through our nostrils, we stimulate this nerve. I learned from Stephen Porges' medical research into the polyvagal system that when we breathe out for at least six seconds, we activate our parasympathetic nervous system. Today, my resting breath rate is six seconds or longer due to years of training and relaxation. You can easily activate your own relaxation response right now by simple extended exhalation breathing practices, singing, or speaking in longer sentences.

I finally know and love myself. I am authentic and honest. I feel connected within and with other people. Social trust is difficult when we know in every cell of our body that people have hurt us and that we cannot trust.

Children require safe, consistent caregiving. When parents are unavailable or abusive, a child experiences feeling unloved and unsafe. Because of the survival level imperative to believe and hope we will be taken care of, we turn that feeling of being unloved into a belief that we are unlovable.

You believe there is something wrong with you because it is too risky as a child to see that the real problem and responsibility lies with the people who are supposed to be taking care of you. These inaccurate core beliefs of unworthiness and being unlovable are at the root of much of our suffering through life. The practices in this book will help you see and dissolve these deficiency stories so you are finally free of them.

My body is relaxed now. I am mostly free of reactivity and I have skills to work with my responses. Trauma I have experienced is largely healed and resolved.

A strong mind has certain characteristics: resilience, endurance, persistence, stillness, less fear and insecurity, wise and kind speech, and the ability to concentrate, to forgive and to believe in oneself and therefore in others.

We develop anxiety and habitual patterns of self-protection based on our experiences. Notice right in this moment if you are safe. If you are not in immediate danger, allow yourself to relax and soften. We don't actually have to stay on alert. We can count on our nervous system to spring into action when needed.

I learned from neuroscience research that our brains have a negativity bias. We evolved to notice danger so our survival system can keep us alive. In today's world, our over-focus on the negative contributes to fear and compulsive thinking. Media, politicians, advertisers, and others play on our fears to manipulate us.

Your efforts to reduce the stressors on your nervous system help immediately. For example, when you add the simple mindfulness practice of focusing for at least thirty seconds on positive experiences, you begin to develop new neural pathways in your brain. Our brains develop in response to both positive and negative experiences; it just takes us longer to notice the good ones.

You **can** make friends with your own mind. Friendliness and inner strength are the foundation for a healthy, fulfilling life. They are the key to freeing yourself from the torture of your thoughts and experiencing a new, more fulfilling way of living.

We have a natural tendency to avoid and turn away from pain. This reflex is managed in our primitive brain and survival system. It is helpful to remember that touching a hot stove will burn us. This same system holds us back when we avoid feeling and connection with others because of past hurt. I know this personally and from working with people who also have learned they can welcome their whole experience.

I no longer feel any aggression toward myself. As the trauma has healed, what remains is compassion and kindness.

I am happy now and I know you can be, too. This is why I work with people who are suffering. I know how to heal from hurt and abuse. I have helped thousands of people learn to meditate, relax, and breathe, and many use the guided practices on my YouTube channel.

I am an expert in helping people identify where they are stuck and being an anchor during their healing journey.

This book will help you understand your mind, body, and nervous system. Knowing how a system works makes it possible to apply an effective remedy when something goes wrong. We develop troubling patterns in response to experiences of fear and stress. They are not permanent.

Good things happen when you face what you have been avoiding. You realize you can tolerate the discomfort, and that even very intense and painful sensations are not here to hurt you. Experiences that were too overwhelming to process at the time they first happened are integrated and naturally release.

You begin to experience life without fear and it becomes possible to relax your vigilance. You discover you are not alone, that you have support, and you can learn how to do this.

I know this to be true from my own direct experience and with other people. Healing is possible and it is worth it.

My Story: PTSD and Recovery

In 2005, I lived across the river from downtown Calgary, Alberta in Canada. I loved riding my bicycle to work, even in the winter. One cold November morning I was cycling on the beautiful pathway along the Bow River when I was physically assaulted. It came out of nowhere, a man running up the river bank. He had no shirt. Shaved head. I had no time to escape. With a couple of running steps, he punched me hard in the side of my head and I flew off the path onto the steep bank of the river. I froze there until I heard a woman screaming. The woman cycling behind me had stopped a few hundred yards ahead, called 911, and screamed for help. Her courage and action saved me.

That began my journey with Post Traumatic Stress Disorder (PTSD). Very little was known about it at the time. I found Dr. Peter Levine's excellent book, Waking The Tiger. I was fortunate to have a psychologist who diagnosed me although I didn't believe her at first. She helped me prepare to testify and she told me the most important thing I needed to know in order to heal.

My nervous system had been traumatized and I needed to experience safety to recover. I had been meditating and doing yoga for a dozen years and as much as I could, I created a sanctuary in my home where I could rest and heal. I did guided relaxation and breathing practices like those you can find on my YouTube Channel. I read and watched movies. Slept. I walked alone in the mountains in grizzly bear country where I felt safer than with people.

It was a long journey to healing. Researching led me to explore and understand Developmental Trauma and now, the events and impact of my teen years began to make sense.

The previous July my son had been misdiagnosed with an aggressive form of lymphoma, with over ninety-five percent of people dying within two years of diagnosis. I was devastated. It was nine weeks before they diagnosed him with mononucleosis and confirmed he did not have cancer.

Between the threats to his life and mine, I began a period of deep reflection about my life, uncovering a lot of confusion, pain, and regret. In 2012, I discovered the Living Inquiries at the same time as I began to learn how childhood trauma affects development in our brains. Medical researchers have learned a tremendous amount about trauma in recent years.

I no longer feel any aggression toward myself. As the trauma healed, what was left was patience, compassion, and kindness.

Through my own journey, I know how our systems work and how to heal from hurt and abuse in our lives. Our work is challenging. The principles are simple to understand. There is hope.

The Surprising Impact of Neglect

Researchers in the Adverse Childhood Experiences Study (ACES) found the developmental impact of neglect to be significant compared to that of abuse, although they often appear together. When essentials such as food and clothing are not provided, we easily recognize this as neglect. It can also be less obvious, like a child who feels disconnected or valued only for their accomplishments and not for who they are as a person.

Mr. Harder was my teacher from Grade Three through Seven. He was a wonderful teacher and I loved him. I worked hard and flourished in his classroom. I didn't get in trouble often but one day in Grade Five, my friend and I got caught breaking a rule and we had to stay after class. He talked calmly with us about it and we had to sit still for ten minutes as punishment. I must have told him after that I was afraid he wouldn't like me anymore. He answered, "Lynn, I don't like you because you always follow the rules. You are lively and smart and fun. I like you because of **who you are**, not for how you behave."

This stands out for me because it was not my experience at home. We knew there was an expectation to do well in school. As was typical of many families in the 1950s, my parents were not very engaged with us as individuals.

Bullying

My best friend moved away the year I turned twelve. I had no one to turn to when my innocence and need for someone to pay attention to me coincided with skipping school with a group of kids including a very popular Grade Twelve boy. Back at school the next day, he bragged about something that didn't happen and I was labeled the "bad girl". I didn't tell anyone what had happened because I was afraid I would be in trouble. My parents didn't seem to notice my distress.

I began to drink and use drugs. When it became too obvious to ignore, my parents sent me away to boarding school in another city.

I had hoped for a fresh start but my reputation preceded me. I gave up, escaping into food, drinking, and drugs. I considered suicide many times during those desperate years.

As a girl in a small town in the midwest of Canada, I could never have dreamed of the blessings and happiness in my life as an adult. Twenty-five years ago when I sat down with my compulsive mind to learn meditation, I could never have dreamed I would be free of that inner voice blaming and judging me for everything I had ever done wrong. And that I would be relaxed and enjoying a meaningful life.

I am so very grateful to have survived that period to the life I have now.

How Thought Works

The mind is a system of stimulus and response. The content of our thoughts is specific to us as individuals. The thought process is universal, common to all human beings. We can understand how thought works and improve the health of the system itself.

Thoughts show up in our minds in two ways: as words, in our inner voice; and in mental images, as pictures or video clips. We respond to thoughts in two ways: with more thoughts, and with sensations, feelings or energy located in our body. Thought is that specific and that simple.

Thoughts are like clouds in the sky in the sense that they come and go. No particular formation of water vapor and air lasts forever. Clouds constantly dissolve and make new forms. The space of the sky is where this is occurring. The sky is not separate from the clouds and it is not changed by what passes through it.

Our brains work a bit differently than the open space of sky in that certain clouds remain as memories. Storm clouds that hurt us are stored as thoughts with feelings in our body. In this way, some thoughts do stay with us.

We have the capacity to shift our perspective from being absorbed in thoughts, to stepping back and noticing the process as it unfolds. We don't control our thoughts and we can't predict them. This is the very nature of thought. Thoughts form in response to our current environment interacting with our pool of memories.

"The answer is to question the mind itself, not to answer its questions."
Scott Kiloby

Parts of the Mind

There are four parts of the mind: our sense of identity, two types of thought, and our storehouse of memories.

We all have a sense of identity. This is how we know who we are.

There are two main layers of thought. We have our regular thoughts about what is happening around us, what we need to do later, and things concerning daily life. We bring information into our brain through our sense perceptions and our brain interprets the data.

The mind is not who we are.
It is an instrument for us to use.

We also have a storehouse of memories. We draw on what we have learned to date in life. When we are stressed or afraid, we can be flooded with fearful and anxious thoughts. When flooded, it is difficult to access our intuition and innate wisdom.

We are wired to notice danger first and our survival system activates instantly to keep us alive. When our alarm system is triggered, our nervous system puts us in a state of yellow or red alert. Our bodies prepare to respond and we may experience intrusive, catastrophic thinking. The activation of our nervous system combined with these fear-based thoughts can be distracting and very compelling.

Many of us are almost completely involved with our thoughts. Like everything we do, there are reasons for this habit. We avoid being present in our bodies with our emotions. We try to figure things out in our minds to avoid our uncomfortable feelings.

A mindfulness practice is to focus on observing our thoughts. In this way we become able to see how the words and images in our mind connect to the physical responses in our body. Mindfulness is a skill and we get better with practice. When we get lost in thought, we notice what has happened, and we step back and observe.

Imagine you are sitting on the bank of a stream. Watch your thoughts and feelings like they are leaves floating by. Some leaves catch in a whirlpool or on the branches of a downed tree. Others flow easily by without obstruction. Thoughts and feelings flow in a similar way.

A strong mind has certain characteristics that we can develop and enhance. The practices in this book are a recipe for a strong mind.

How the Brain Works

This book focuses on the processes of the mind rather than the workings of the brain itself, but they are certainly connected. It is helpful to know some basics of neurobiology. Researchers now have the technology to understand more about our brains and how they function.

One recent discovery is that our brains have neuroplasticity. They change and grow throughout our life. This is wonderful news, especially for people whose brain development was affected by trauma.

Neurons that fire together wire together

Our brains are complex electrical systems. Activity in the neurons, called firing, is connected via synapses that are wired together into a network. Neural pathways and networks form based on our experience.

Our brain is always "on" and hard at work. Activity is lightning fast and we are not aware of most of it in our conscious mind. Information is fed to the brain through our nervous system and sense perceptions. Eighty percent of the messages between the brain and our body come from the gut to the brain.

The brain stem connects to our spinal cord and is the most primitive part of our brain. It governs survival functions of heart rate, breathing, digestion, and sleep.

The amygdala is part of the primitive brain and is deep within the limbic emotional brain. It is alert to survival needs, including sex and to emotional reactions like anger and fear. It reacts immediately, well before our prefrontal cortex responds.

The prefrontal cortex is the most recently evolved area of our brain and is the seat of our executive function. It guides behavior, deals with complex issues, and adapts to new data. It is the last part of the brain to develop.

Our brains have a bias toward survival over happiness. Our primitive brain areas can hijack our more evolved thinking brain, even taking it offline for a period of time. Understanding the basics of our brain and nervous system helps us function more effectively in life.

Negativity Bias in the Brain

Our survival system is set up so we pay attention to what could threaten our life. It is in our best interest to notice danger more than positive events. Yet this also contributes to negative thinking patterns.

The negativity bias of the brain means that danger is noticed immediately and positive experiences are not. A mindfulness practice of deliberate focus on positive experiences for several seconds gives the brain time to notice and respond. Neural pathways develop in our brain based on experience and is part of how we form associations.

"The brain is like Velcro for negative experiences, but Teflon for positive ones."
Dr. Rick Hanson, Ph.D

Stop and use all your senses to pay attention to pleasurable experiences. Someone you love comes home. You stop what you are doing and let your happiness in seeing them show on your face. Greet them. Really look at them. Notice the expression on their face and their body language. If you give them a hug, let yourself notice how they feel and smell. Immerse yourself in the experience for at least thirty seconds.

Mindfully attending to positive experiences can help to balance our system's automatic focus on danger and can remind us that happiness is here, too. My meditation teacher would often remind us to look for what there is to enjoy in a situation and to focus on that.

How Feelings Work

We live in a culture uncomfortable with intense feelings. Unprocessed emotion can lead to feeling numb or disconnected. Present events can remind us of the distress of unhealed early events. Working with thoughts and feelings through the mindfulness practices and exercises in this book will radically transform your relationship with your own emotions.

> **"Rather than feeling directly, we are used to thinking about how we feel."**
> **Scott Kiloby**

We feel emotions as energy or sensation in our body. Feelings too overwhelming to process at the time they happened are stored in our tissues with associated memories, words that were said, and mental pictures of the incident.

The Living Inquiries are a method with which we look individually at words, images, and sensation to release their Velcro, the associations of memories with feelings. In this way, we process stored emotion from our past and allow it to heal.

Emotional Flooding

When we feel threatened, a flood of hormones and chemicals jump into action to engage our survival system. These include cortisol and adrenaline, necessary for fight-or-flight. It takes about twenty-five minutes for these hormones to clear our body. During this time, we have little access to our thinking brain, the prefrontal cortex.

When you are flooded and in fight/flight/ freeze mode, you will do whatever is necessary to protect yourself because it feels life-threatening. As you learn the signs, you can recognize when this is happening to you. You might suggest taking a break from a discussion or go for a walk while you allow your system to down-regulate.

Many of us live in chronic states of stress where our survival mechanisms are stuck on yellow alert. Persistently high levels of stress hormones can result in serious negative consequences both to our health and in our relationships.

Some people disengage when they are flooded. This is frustrating for the other person and it eventually leads to a lack of intimacy and connection.

For some people, the pattern is to lash out when they are triggered. They might be rude and cutting, or fly into a rage.

It can feel like there is very little control over these responses and, in the moment, that can be true. Longer term, inquiry into what triggers us will help reduce our "hot buttons". Our capacity to recognize the signs of emotional flooding increases as the intensity of the trigger decreases.

If a rain barrel is almost full, it takes very little additional water to trigger an overflow. Working consistently with breathing and relaxation practices helps us to lower our resting level of stress.

Avoiding Intense Sensation

The intensity of an emotion or sensation in our body can be misinterpreted as a threat to us. If it feels as though there is a hurtful or threatening intention in a sensation, how do you know that? When we look as we do in the Living Inquiries, we may see words and images as we first pay attention to the sensation. As they begin to fall away, we often begin to notice that the sensation is here to warn and/or protect us. It indicates there is trauma stored in our body.

This is a normal part of our alert system. We can acknowledge and respect we have a system that remembers harm and tries to protect us. This is a good thing!

Most of us usually pull back from intense sensation and try to control or numb our feelings. We have not experienced the sensations in our bodies in a confident way where we pay attention to what is happening and glean the information it has for us, without it feeling intolerable.

It is natural for us to attempt to avoid feeling hurt, afraid, and unsafe. What triggers these feelings in our everyday life depends in part on our early childhood experiences. We are all in human bodies and we have nervous systems. We are hardwired to remember danger.

Confidence builds as we experience for ourselves that our feelings are not here to hurt us. In fact, they have tried to protect us. As we are present with the sensations in our body, we discover we can benefit from feeling them.

What would happen if you went into the sensation and paid attention to it? This practice definitely gets easier with time and repetition because we develop confidence that we can stay with our feelings. Turning away from emotions and feelings is the root of addiction and of distraction behaviors like excessive screen time, eating, or shopping. Turning toward the sensations in our own bodies and feeling our own feelings is healing.

Here is a personal experience that illustrates this. Colette Kelso was a Senior Facilitator of the Living Inquiries. We had been working together for about six months and I trusted her. I was also gradually beginning to trust I would be okay staying with whatever thoughts and emotions were coming up.

During a session on a traumatic incident from my teen years, I had a sharp, intense pain in my heart. It lasted about three minutes, during which time I noticed it, stayed with it, breathed into it, and observed it. Some memories came up and I looked at those but it was mostly me paying attention and breathing. After a few minutes the intensity lessened and the pain gradually dissolved.

I thought "Wow, I've been avoiding that three minutes of pain for fifty years! How many pints of ice cream have I eaten to stop myself from feeling this?"

I felt it and I survived feeling it. This was the beginning of freedom for me. I knew I could stay with any pain that was ready to come up. I could attend to myself. It was a big breakthrough.

We can take the perspective of an observer more easily with words and images than we can with sensation because its energy is inside our body and can feel frightening or disorienting. We can see words and images "in our mind's eye" but sensation is inside our body and is real and felt in the moment.

We often have a whole lifetime of practicing distraction to avoid our feelings. It takes courage to stay and feel what is going on in our hearts, throats, and guts. For each of us, this is our own hero's journey.

How to Stay with Your Feelings

Observe an uncomfortable sensation in your body. Is there something physical about it? Does it hurt or feel like fire? What is it specifically that makes it feel painful, scary or threatening?

How would you describe the feeling to a scientist recording your experience? Is it hot or cold? Dense and still? Pulsing? Expanding? Does it have a color? Are there clearly defined edges or does it dissipate gradually? What is its shape?

Notice the space around the sensation. Track it to the edges and notice where the sensation "isn't". Does it go to the edges of your body or is it only in the middle? Can you feel it in your chest or up into your throat? Can you feel it a foot in front of you? Notice all the space around it where you can't feel the sensation. As intense as a feeling can be, it does not extend infinitely. There is an edge or ending to it.

Do you have an image of the sensation? Some people have more visual minds than others and it is common for them to see an image. Look at that as you would any image. See if you can put it into a picture frame with empty space around the image. When a sensation feels overwhelming or all-consuming, it can be the image that adds to the intensity.

When we are able to find a way to be present with the feelings and energies that are in our body, we begin to unwind the memories and associations causing these thoughts to feel threatening.

There is more to our feelings than our thoughts about how we feel. There is also the direct experience of how we feel. If you are sad right now, sadness is also a sensation in your body and you can feel that.

Working with Feelings

Remember to breathe and do not push yourself. Cultivate a relaxed invitation to be present.

Notice the qualities and attributes of the sensation, including color, temperature, shape, size, density or lightness, sharp or diffuse boundaries, and noticing if it is still or moving.

Does it feel like this is here to hurt you? If yes, how do you know that? Are there words and images attached?

Notice if there is an unkind or mean intention, or if you have a sense that it wants to hurt you. If yes, work with the words and images that give you that sense.

Notice the location of the feeling. Where exactly in your body do you feel it? For example, we might have a sensation like a fist in our gut, right behind our belly button.

Notice where the feeling is and is not. Where are the edges? If you feel it in your chest, does it move up into your throat?

See if you can put your attention right into the very center of the sensation, like you are experiencing it from the inside.

Direct attention might feel unwelcome. If so, notice the edges of the sensation and the space all around it. Use your peripheral vision.

Mining is a way to explore what a sensation means. There are a series of questions that you direct to the sensation to help you to look more deeply.

What does this sensation mean? What are you afraid of? What are you ashamed of? What is connected to you (the sensation)? When was this first created? What is it protecting me from?

Do this with an open curiosity and wait to see what comes up. You are not trying to figure anything out with your thinking mind. You are mining the sensation to see the words and images that are associated with the feeling. The right question can unlock a lot of unconscious material.

Painful and intense energy in our body is stored trauma and emotion that felt overwhelming at the time it first happened. What feels safe enough to feel now will come forward to be seen and healed.

Honor and respect your own defense mechanisms. When you feel safe, your defense mechanisms will stand down and go off duty.

Fearful and Anxious Thoughts

Certain thoughts command our attention to the exclusion of other layers and nuances of our human experience. We have all been distracted or pulled into a train of thought. It happens in those times when we are sitting with nothing to do and it also happens while we are watching television or even talking with a friend.

> "The key is to shift from
> thinking to looking at thought,
> from thinking to hearing words."
> **Scott Kiloby**

Being hijacked by our thoughts makes it difficult to fully engage with people and with our lives. Being overly involved with our thoughts can also be a way to avoid uncomfortable feelings.

Thoughts linked with intense feelings and sensations are often associated with stories we have repeated to ourselves through the years. They feel so true and so core to us that it can be hard to shift our perspective about them.

Anxiety is common in modern culture and drives many of the patterns of thinking and avoidance discussed in this book. We need to calm our nervous systems and lower our anxiety for it to be possible to stop torturing ourselves with our thoughts.

It is difficult for others to be around us when we are anxious. People sense this type of energy and it can trigger their own anxiety. People may avoid us because they sense neediness. We are desperately unhappy and may look to others to help us.

Anxiety drives behaviors that cause us to suffer and make us feel worse. We might be overly critical of ourselves and others, leading us to hurt both ourselves and the people we love. Engaging in gossip is another example of a way to feel included and powerful but leaves us feeling uneasy, and unsure if we will be targeted next.

There are many ways this plays out in our lives. You can learn about and understand the basic system of how this works. You can heal and recover. This is possible for all of us.

"The process of spotting fear and refusing to obey it is the source of all true empowerment."

Martha Beck

Deficiency Stories and (Inaccurate) Core Beliefs

A deficiency story or core belief is formed early in life and involves negative judgments about ourselves. Common deficiency stories include "I am unlovable", "I'm stupid" and "I'm not good enough". In situations of neglect or abuse, a child's need for safety and love makes it too risky for them to question or blame their parents. Children turn their criticism inward in an attempt to make sense of their situation.

This mechanism of self-blame can occur in any situation where a child is left to fend for themselves in and outside of the family.

In the example below, the child's internalized experience is very different from that of her parents.

Colleen and Dave have a seven-year-old daughter, Leia. They both have good jobs but Dave's employer is laying off twenty percent of employees. Dave works long hours trying to prove his worth to the company. His mother died of an aneurism a year ago and he will soon need to get more help for his father who is in early stages of Alzheimer's. His father is lonely, Dave feels guilty his wife is picking up more than her share at home, and work is a pressure cooker.

Colleen's job is secure but she has a heavy workload. Leia had always come home from school to her grandparents and misses them. Leia alternates between being clingy and blowing up with the sitters. She wants to see her grandfather after school and doesn't understand why she can't.

Colleen tries to be home to make supper but is distracted by email and texts from work and finds herself irritated by Leia's whining. She works for a few hours after Leia is in bed then is up at 5:30 to start the routine again.

We can understand the pressures on the parents and also that Leia could feel unloved. Memories of being cared for by her grandparents are becoming dimmer. Her experience now is one of feeling isolated and on her own.

A deficiency story develops when the feeling of being unloved turns into a core belief: "I'm unlovable". Every time in life that Leia is ignored or feels unloved, it becomes further evidence for the belief that she is inherently unlovable.

No parent attends perfectly to their children and none of us has all our needs met. When this happens to us as children frequently and over a long period of time, it reinforces the belief that there is something wrong with us.

Evidence accumulates through experiencing feeling a certain way. When practicing the Living Inquiries, we examine the evidence we have for our core beliefs.

This mechanism of turning against ourselves can be extreme, leading to feelings of loathing, unworthiness, and self-hatred. We blame ourselves for harm others did to us.

Event: *Someone hurt and abused me.*

Incorrect conclusion: *They abused me because I am disgusting. I deserved it.*

People who abuse others are trying to avoid their own pain. They make the person they abused feel it is their fault through gaslighting, pretending it is not abuse or is no big deal. They threaten you if you tell the secret. They make you believe the reason they did it is because there is something wrong with you, not with them.

Reframe: *The person who abused me is responsible, not me. I was traumatized by the experience. Everyone deserves safety and protection, including me. I had no way at the time to understand this. I do now. I can be kind with myself and support my own healing.*

This has been rigorously researched. To survive into adulthood, we need the care and protection of our family. When that is not our experience, our nervous system responds in predictable ways.

Through working with the Living Inquiries, I was able to see that as a teenager I frequently experienced feeling neglected and unloved. It was an experience; it was not who I was. When I acted out and tried to avoid the pain of feeling abandoned through drinking, drugs, and other behaviors, I was not a "bad girl". I was a young person alone, confused, and trying to feel better.

> *"Owning our story can be hard*
> *but not nearly as difficult as spending*
> *our lives running from it. "*
> **Brené Brown**

I Have Experienced

Try adding "I have experienced" to the beginning of some phrases. If you are looking at a core belief of "**I am unlovable**", also look at these two sentences:

> **"I have had the experience of feeling unloved."**

> **"I have had the experience of feeling loved."**

We change our perspective when we see these words are describing a way we sometimes feel based on our experiences.

Remembering we have had both positive and negative experiences helps to overcome the brain's negativity bias.

Does the experience of feeling unloved really mean what we believe it to mean? That we are unlovable? Then what does it mean that you have also had the experience of feeling loved?

The Velcro Effect

We have thoughts that feel neutral emotionally. Other thoughts result in a positive or negative emotional reaction and are also felt as energy in our body. Neutral thoughts come and go through our mind. They don't "land" and they don't generate other thoughts or feelings.

Bring to mind a baby giggling or you relaxing on a beach and pay attention to the warm feeling inside your body. Now bring to mind something you perceive as scary. Fearful or negative thoughts generate a different kind of sensation or feeling inside the body.

Scott Kiloby uses the term Velcro Effect to describe the way thoughts that are connected to feelings and sensation in our body feel more true and inherently real. In his method, the Living Inquiries, we look at three different elements of experience.

The three elements are: the words we think; pictures or images in our mind's eye; and sensation, energy or feelings in our body.

"Bring your attention into whatever emotion
or sensation you're feeling, and without words,
feel into it.

Begin to notice the space around it.
It's hanging out in space,
like the moon hangs out in the night sky."
Scott Kiloby

The Power of Words

Words mean something to us and about us. They interact with our memories and feelings in our body. Through paying particular attention to the words we hear and think (in our inner voice), we can diminish their negative effects. Try this mindfulness practice exploring your experience with neutral, positive, and negative words.

Working with Words

We hear sounds, vibrations and words (our audible or inner voice). Notice the sound itself, the tone of voice.

See the words in your "mind's eye" or see them on a blank page. Notice the font, color, and size of the letters. Notice the spaces in and around the letters.

What happens when you change the font, size, color, and spacing of the words? Bold black lettering feels more intense than lighter letters.

Try making the letters into animated characters. The words don't feel as threatening.

See words clearly then notice what happens if you let them become blurry or foggy.

If words feel particularly powerful, open your eyes. Write them down and look at them.

With your eyes open, place the words on a window. Notice the letters and also the sky and space behind the words. Words are letters and shapes.

Trace the space around the words. Put the words in a frame and focus on the space outside of the frame. Let your eyes move slowly around the frame clockwise then counterclockwise a few times then look back at the words. Repeat if you like.

The Power of Images

Bring up a happy or neutral childhood memory and notice whether you are looking at the scene as though you are still a child, seeing it through your eyes as it appeared to you then.

Now, try taking a step back and look at the same scene as though you are watching it on a screen through your adult eyes. Taking a step back makes it is easier to realize we are looking at a memory. The incident is not happening now. It is possible to bring up painful memories of the past without retraumatizing ourselves.

Working with Images

We usually see images with our eyes closed, in our "mind's eye". This can feel quite real, like it is actually happening.

Look out of your own eyes at the scene. This feels close in, like you are there.

Take a step back and see yourself as well, as though you are watching from the edge of the scene. This gives you more distance.

Put a frame around the image like a picture or like you are seeing a video clip on a screen. There is even more distance now.

Move the image from the center of your vision to a corner so it doesn't fill the whole space.

Open your eyes and see the image on a wall. It becomes clear this isn't happening right now. Do this whenever the image is persistent or too threatening to look at with your eyes closed. This helps us remain aware that we are looking at images, not experiencing an event.

Notice the space between you and the image and the space all around the image. This makes it easier to see you are looking at an image. You could have more responses to the image of other thoughts or sensations. This is natural.

Look at the image with a frame around it. Moving your eyes, trace the space around the outside of the image clockwise three times, then in the opposite direction. When you are finished tracing the space, look back at the picture and notice your response.

If you are seeing many images, you can bring one into focus or you can put them all onto a collage like they are on a poster board. Work with the collage of pictures as a whole like you would with a single image.

Thoughts are Attached or Velcroed to Body Sensation

The power of the Living Inquiries is that we slow down and look at the individual elements that combine to create our experience. The three elements - words, pictures, and sensation - are part of the stimulus-response process of the mind.

Humans have a mind and a nervous system. We are hardwired to notice danger first. We draw on our experience. This is how our system works to protect us.

Let's look at an example based on a common fear. Most people are more afraid of public speaking than they are of dying.

"I have to give a speech next week".

Facilitator: What comes to mind when you look at those words?

I'll forget what I'm going to say.

Facilitator: Look at the letters, like they are written out on a blank page. Look at the color, the font, the shapes of the letters. Listen to the sound vibration. Can those words hurt you?

No, but I can see a picture of me standing on the stage. I have a blank look on my face and I'm sweating.

Facilitator: Look at the colors and shapes that make up that image. Notice the details. Can that picture you're looking at hurt you?

Yes.

Facilitator: How is it you know that? Is it something about the colors or shapes? The look on your face?

I'm not sure how I know. It just feels threatening. If I forget the words I'll look like a fool.

Facilitator: Is there a sensation or feeling in your body?

There is! My shoulders are up around my ears. I just noticed I'm holding my breath. Relaxes and takes a deep breath.

Facilitator: Let's look at those words. "I'll look like a fool". Are those words you, the fool?

I'm not the words exactly but something about them makes me feel uncomfortable. I feel a bit queasy in my stomach.

During an inquiry, we keep looking at words, pictures, and feelings, one at a time until the power in them dissolves. There are no right or wrong answers. Words are sounds and shapes. Images are colors and shapes. It is the Velcro of words and images to sensations in our body that makes thought feel real or true.

Working with sensations, we realize they are not here to hurt us. Knowing this about the feelings in our body is what makes it possible to allow them in. We become able to turn toward what has been driving anxiety and suffering most of our lives.

Stored trauma is seen, felt, and dissolves. Unresolved issues are brought into the present as words we hear, images we see, and feelings in our body. With trauma, it is essential to work with a trained, skillful and safe facilitator at first. When a person decides to finally face and feel the pain that they may have been avoiding for years or decades, the first steps cannot be done alone.

As we do these mindfulness practices, we are no longer a mystery to ourselves. We know how our system works. We have confidence in these effective tools that have brought positive change to our lives. This is all we need.

Catastrophic Thought

Compulsive Intrusive Thinking

Compelling thoughts have the power to take us away from the present moment. They trigger feelings of fear and anxiety, showing up like a storm in our system. Think of times you've been ruminating, compulsively going over something in your mind. This type of thought often relates to a past event that you wish was different or anxiety about what may happen in the future.

These are the thoughts that keep us from sleeping at night. This is the racing mind that never lets us rest. It is important to recognize the negative effects on our brain, nervous system, and lives when these gain momentum and begin to predominate in our mind.

As a culture we are beginning to be aware of the harmful effects of sports concussions and to protect young players through policies like mandatory helmet use. Compulsively banging our head is harmful, whether it is against a wall or a soccer ball. Let's be clear that compulsive, negative thinking also hurts us.

There are healthy and effective strategies for helping to slow down your thoughts, including breathing and relaxation exercises, going for a walk, or immersing yourself in a project. Reading a book out loud can break the momentum. Develop a list that works for you.

Effective but unhealthy strategies with disastrous consequences are distractions and addictions so prevalent in our culture. These include shopping, binge watching on Netflix, compulsive cleaning or addictions like gambling, sex, food, and alcohol or other drugs.

We can change and heal this pattern.

Ruminating: Next time I'll …

At times we have trouble accepting how something turned out. It could be a conversation in which we couldn't think of the right thing to say, then on the way home, a great response comes to us. We replay the event, seeing it in our mind's eye, and feeling the satisfaction of having the perfect comeback.

This type of ruminating thought can give us an instant replay with a different outcome than what actually happened. Why do we need to go over some things until we "get it right"? And why weren't we able to think of a powerful response on the spot?

You may have been a bit nervous or shut down at the time. The lack of a snappy comeback might indicate something about your nervous system but it doesn't have to define you.

You may have avoided saying something because of fear or uncertainty. When you are relaxed and on your own later, the response comes. By replaying it in detail in your mind, you can experience the comfort of having a positive resolution.

What-If Catastrophic Thinking

Catastrophic thoughts generate fear in our body. When we are scared, these thoughts come forward in an attempt to prepare ourselves for all eventualities. Most people are familiar with worry about a possible car crash when someone we love is late returning home. Parents look at their sleeping child and fear the worst. Strong emotional connections contribute to the urgent feeling or need to take immediate action.

This is compulsive, catastrophic thinking

Catastrophic thinking and planning is an attempt to make ourselves feel better. It often starts with an unlikely but possible scenario so vividly imagined we experience it in our bodies as though it is true.

We have this persistent idea that if we could just figure things out, we would have a plan to stay safe no matter what happens.

Catastrophic thoughts pull us into a storm of fear and anxiety. With this intensity in our thoughts, our prefrontal cortex, our thinking brain, is less available. Like a boat on an ocean in a storm, the waves on the surface feel as though they require all of our attention to deal with the emergency at hand.

It is unhealthy for our mind and body to go along with catastrophic thinking. The pressure builds and hormones flood our systems. We can immobilize ourselves through the way our mind is working.

At times we have good evidence that our catastrophic thoughts could come true.

This makes the thoughts feel real and inspires a need to take action. We spin off into thoughts, what about this, and what-if that ... This is actually not helpful. It stimulates fear in the mind that builds on itself and creates confusion.

Several strategies help to ease catastrophic thinking. This is the time to breathe, relax, and practice good self-care. Rest, exercise, good nutrition, and sleep help down-regulate our nervous system and improve the functioning of our mind.

Use the Living Inquiries and see thoughts as they come in as pictures made up of colors and shapes. Ask yourself, "Can that image actually hurt me?"

Even when there is a high probability something negative or harmful could happen, our thoughts about that possibility are still images and words that trigger a feeling in our body.

When my son was misdiagnosed with an aggressive form of cancer, he had a deep mindfulness practice of looking in the present moment to see if he was dying right then. He might find pain or fatigue at times and often there would just be breathing in and out. It is the thoughts in our mind that create such intensity that we feel we need to escape. When he told me how he was working with it, I began to do the same.

Two things happen when we have the experience of being able to stay with and feel our uncomfortable emotions. One is that we realize we can tolerate intense feelings. The other is that when we have a willingness and capacity to feel all emotion and sensation, this allows them to pass through. We don't have to numb out or escape into addiction, anger or bliss.

This is our human life. It can be very hard. We may have times of being terrified. It helps to have compassion for ourselves, remembering that this is how it is. We can give ourselves the room to have our full experience.

Kindness and Truth

We need both kindness towards ourselves and a willingness for reflection and truth to make friends with our own minds.

Kindness includes being compassionate and friendly within. Truth involves clear seeing, an open curiosity, and is without denial, judgment or shaming. Often we don't realize we are being cruel to ourselves.

What interferes with clear sight and kindness?

Perfectionism may inform your ideas of how you should be. Pushing and shaming yourself does not lead to positive change. It makes it harder. It is a relief to become aware of your "shoulds" and to begin to let go of impossible standards.

It can be quite a practice to forgive. Forgiveness does not mean we condone wrong action. It does mean that we stop retroactively judging and shaming ourselves based on what we know now but were not aware of at the time.

Acceptance is a precursor to forgiveness and clear seeing. We understand why we have behaved as we have. We forgive ourselves for being human. We make amends as best we can. We deserve to be happy and have a meaningful, engaged life.

Condemning and being cruel to ourselves does not help anyone. Healing ourselves is the very best contribution we can make to the lives of those we love. We then become available to them in ways that are not possible when we are stuck in a shame spiral about our past.

We practice kindness and compassion for ourselves and each other. Seeing this inspires people around us to know healing is a possibility for them too. Systematically we let go of the barriers. The kindness and compassion that is our true nature shines through.

It is so helpful to acknowledge we are suffering and to offer solace to ourselves. This can be as simple as putting a hand on our heart and feeling the warmth. This is a good basis for deepening friendship.

Off the Hamster Wheel

The first step in personal change or growth is awareness. Stop and acknowledge your compulsive or catastrophic thinking. Notice when you are unkind to yourself. These are your thoughts. You can understand and observe what happens in your own mind.

I know what happens when I follow that train of thought. What can I do in this moment to stop doing what hurts me?

In this way, we create a bit of breathing room and see that we are trying to feel better and be more functional. We understand why we've adopted our current strategies. They worked at one time. If they are no longer effective, we can try a different strategy or let go of them entirely.

We developed unhealthy thought patterns as a response to our environment. When we change our thoughts, we can become mentally healthy. I know because I have done it. I know from the Living Inquiries, and from teaching meditation to thousands of people, what a game-changer it is to heal our minds.

The key to dealing with compulsive and catastrophic thinking is to slow down, step back, and change your perspective. Observe thought as it comes in. We are so much more than the content of our thoughts, no matter how compelling they seem. We have a higher level of our mind that is able to observe and witness our life.

Let's look at a recent experience of Heather as an example of how this could all come together:

> Yesterday at work I got an email from my boss about my upcoming performance review. I notice it has been coming into my thoughts repeatedly since then. Something about it is bugging me.
>
> I look at the words of his email in my mind's eye like I'm seeing them on my computer screen. In one sentence halfway through, the print looks heavy, darker, and kind of menacing.

When I look at the words in that sentence, I can see it's no longer the words. I have a tight jaw and my teeth are clenched, like I'm holding back from saying what I feel. I put a bit of space between my upper and lower jaw and take a few deep breaths.

I scan my body. There is an uneasy feeling in my stomach as I look at my boss's email. I feel nauseous and like something is flipping around in there.

I can see it's not the shapes of the letters that are making me uncomfortable, it's the rolling sensation in my stomach. It reminds me of the dread I used to feel in school waiting for my marks.

Heather can now go on to pay attention to the sensation itself and look at other words and images that come up as it plays itself out. Until our emotions are felt in our bodies, as well as replayed in our thoughts, they may persist or be triggered by current events in life.

Understanding and feeling our emotions allows us to heal from these automatic responses that cause so much suffering.

Letting Our Guard Down

Many of us have a fear of relaxing fully. We are habitually on guard. It is often felt as tightness through the back of our neck, shoulders, and upper back or a knot of fear in the belly. This contraction is especially hard to release when our life experience has proven to us that we must stay vigilant to protect ourselves and be prepared for appropriate action. When this persists over a period of time, it becomes a habit in our nervous system and muscles.

Some people have a sense of personal safety and they develop confidence that they will be okay. They know how to self-soothe and regulate their nervous system when they are stressed or upset.

Some people have the direct experience of harm and not being safe. We have that "knowing" in our nervous system. We may not have learned as children how to self-soothe and down-regulate our nervous system. We are not certain we will be okay.

A benefit of resting and attending to your internal sensations is that you can see there is no immediate threat in your environment. The habit of vigilance that developed from your life experiences has become a default. Check in and see if it is necessary to protect yourself right now. If you don't need to defend yourself in this moment, then relax your protective mechanism and let your muscles soften.

We can wear ourselves out by constant vigilance. The result is less resilience when we do need to act. We can trust our survival system to spring into action if and when it is needed. At all other times, it helps to breathe and relax.

Breathe, Relax, Heal

Our bodies and nervous systems are affected by both negative and positive events and experiences in our lives. Over time, our responses become hardwired in our bodies and become automatic patterns.

Have you noticed you hold your breath when you're scared? Our survival system steps in when we need a big gasp of air to prepare for fight/flight/freeze.

Chronic anxiety creates an ongoing pattern of holding our breath. This is damaging to our heart muscle and heightens our stress.

Smooth and continuous diaphragmatic breathing is a simple and powerful way to make an immediate change in our nervous system and emotional state.

Right now, tune in to your body. Notice if there is tightness in your forehead and eyebrows. Soften the hinges of your jaw and let go if you are clenching your teeth. Relax your neck and allow your shoulders to settle down away from your ears. Release any contraction in the large muscles of your upper back. Put a hand on your stomach and allow your muscles to lengthen as you breathe in and settle as you breathe out.

Many people tell me they are not comfortable paying attention to sensations and feelings in their body. The lovely, deep guided breathing and relaxation practices of yoga meditation allow for safe "re-entry".

"Bring your mind in from other times and places, rest your attention on your Being." Pandit Dabral

Yoga, Qi Gong and Tai Chi are three gentle ways to work with and become familiar with our body. The Living Inquiries are a way to release stored trauma, opening up space to inhabit and enjoy our bodies.

I have recorded many guided relaxation and breathing practices that will help.

Fear and Anxiety in Daily Life

The Anxiety Inquiry

Go to www.FriendsWithYourMind.com to listen to a guided Anxiety Inquiry practice.

All of the Living Inquiries look at three elements - words, images, and sensations - and ask one of three questions. The Unfindable Inquiry asks, "Is that word, image, or sensation me?" The Compulsion Inquiry asks, "Is there an urge or drive to do something on that word, image, or in the sensation?"

The question we use in the Anxiety Inquiry is, "where is the threat?" We can also look for what is making us feel uncomfortable, what seems scary or terrifying or what feels like it is putting us in danger.

When practicing the Anxiety Inquiry, choose the wording that fits best for you.

Here is a short example of an inquiry into feeling threatened about not having enough money.

Start with your thoughts that are showing up as words in your mind. In this example we will use Tara's concern: "I don't have enough money to retire. I am going to be homeless."

Facilitator: Look at words in your mind's eye. Sometimes it helps to see them as though they are printed on an empty page in a book.

The words are "I don't have enough money to retire. I am going to be homeless."

Facilitator: Do the words themselves feel threatening?

Yes, there's something about the word "homeless". It's darker than the rest.

An image of a bag lady just popped into my mind. It's me. I'm about 75. I'm pushing a cart containing some torn garbage bags. My feet are cold and wet. My head is down and all I can see is my cart and people's feet.

Facilitator: Take a step back and notice if you can see yourself in the scene too. Instead of looking down at your cart out of your own eyes, can you look at it as an image of yourself as a bag lady with a cart?

Yes, I can do that. I look about 90.

Facilitator: Does that picture of you as a bag lady with your cart feel threatening? Remember there are no right or wrong answers. If you have a response in your body or it stimulates other thoughts, it's a yes.

Yes. There is a tight knot of fear in my stomach.

Facilitator: Let's focus on that sensation. Can you describe where it is and what it feels like?

It's a few inches behind my belly button. It is dark and pulsing, like it's trying to pull me in.

Facilitator: Do you have an image of it? If so, can you pull it up and have a look at it like a picture?

I do. It looks like a slowly spinning black hole that gets darker and darker in the middle.

Facilitator: Look at the colors and shapes in the image. Does the picture itself feel threatening? Could it hurt you?

Yes. It feels like it could pull me in and I'd disappear.

Facilitator: Can you put it into a frame and see some space around the edges?

Not really. It keeps flipping back to take up the whole space.

Facilitator: Let's try it with your eyes open. Put the picture onto a blank section of wall across the room. Notice the space between you and the picture. Notice you can still see the wall behind it.

Yes. It still seems like it can pull me in. It's scary.

Facilitator: Can you see space around the edges of the picture? Can you focus your eyes there?

Yes, if I focus on the space outside of the frame, it helps. I can breathe better.

Facilitator: Trace the space and let your eyes move around it clockwise two or three times then counterclockwise. Take your time. When you're done, look back at the picture. Is the picture itself scary?

No. I can see it's just a picture.

Facilitator: Bring your attention back to the sensation in your belly. Describe what is happening there now.

I can feel an energy there. It's not as intense.

Facilitator: Does it feel like it would be okay to put your attention right into the center of the sensation, in that space behind your belly button?

Yes.

Facilitator: Let's give it some time. Let me know if any images or words come up. We'll have a look at them.

This is a shortened version of an Anxiety Inquiry with the basic steps. Tara would continue to look at other words and images associated with the sensations.

Fear of Flying

Jason is terrified of flying and is on a plane several times a year for work. He experienced two separate trips three years ago during which there was engine trouble. Both planes landed safely. After the second near-miss, he had a panic attack on his next trip just as the crew was preparing to take off. The passenger beside him and a flight attendant helped him calm down enough so he could stay on the flight. The next day he got a prescription for Xanax from his doctor. It helps but he feels weak having to rely on medication.

When Jason thinks of flying, he is flooded with thoughts like these: "I have a bad feeling about this. This plane is going to crash." "What if the engines start on fire?" "Did the pilots get enough sleep last night?" These are just some of the thoughts running through his mind that create the panic and fear. He also worries about having another panic attack.

Jason is in a bind. He can understand his mind and system reacting this way because he has had the direct experience of something going wrong on a flight. Statistics asserting the relative safety of air flight don't help much because the threat is in his survival system which doesn't respond well to reasoning and rational thought. Shaming himself into staying on the plane might keep him in his seat but it does not dissolve the underlying drive to flee danger.

He wants to resolve his fear of flying permanently and uses the Anxiety Inquiry to look at words, phrases and images. Jason asks himself "Is this a danger or threat?" He notices he feels the fear in his body and looks to see if the sensation is the threat in and of itself. He sees thoughts and sensations are actually separate even though they show up together.

It is when we are able to look for the threat in each element - words, images, and sensations - and see that none of them on their own can hurt us, that the fear dissolves. Try the Anxiety Inquiry yourself and see what it reveals.

A helpful step in healing anxiety related to flying is that when you are calm, write out a list of what to remember when you feel yourself starting to escalate.

What is on the list? Your strategies to down-regulate your nervous system arousal. Write your list on an index card or put it on your phone. Have your list easy to access and refer to it before you get on the plane.

Why is it important to write a list when you are not panicking and to keep it with you? When you are anxious your system goes into fight/flight/freeze and is flooded with survival hormones like adrenaline and cortisol. Our prefrontal cortex, the thinking part of our brain, can go offline for about twenty-five minutes.

It helps to practice key parts of your plan, like relaxing and breathing, ahead of time. This will give you more stability plus you'll start out more relaxed.

Regular work with the skills of breathing and relaxation has two benefits. Our nervous system is healthier and more resilient and additionally, it occurs to us to take a deep breath and relax when we are stressed.

Pre-flight Checklist

You've prepared your list when you were calm. You have it on your phone or print it and keep it with you.

Plan to get to the airport in plenty of time to avoid the stress of rushing.

Take several deep breaths. Rest one hand on your stomach to remind yourself to relax as you breathe out.

Do a breathing practice like continuous smooth breathing, extended exhalations of six seconds, or box breathing. My YouTube Channel and FriendsWithYourMind.com have guided practices and other resources.

Relax your forehead and consciously let go of worry. Soften your jaw and shoulders.

Check to see if the person next to you would be suitable to talk to and distract yourself with an engaging conversation.

Keep breathing and relaxing. Let thoughts be in the back of your mind. As soon as you notice you are following fearful thoughts into a rabbit hole, come back and focus on breathing. Relax your forehead, jaw, back of the neck and shoulders, and your stomach.

Social Anxiety

Children literally cannot survive without the protection and resources of their parents. As we grow, we require food, shelter, and a secure attachment to our caregivers. We need to be protected from harm and abuse.

The Adverse Childhood Experiences Study (ACES) was first done in the mid-1990s with consistent results in the years since. Researchers were shocked by the prevalence of childhood trauma and abuse and the lifelong negative impact on a person's mental and physical health, finances, and exposure to violence.

Most of the hurt we experience as children comes at the hands of other people. A result of having been mistreated, neglected or abused during our early years is that we may more easily feel victimized by certain people or situations in our adult lives. Our nervous system records potential danger and our survival system activates to protect us from other people. We often feel safer alone.

What to do now, especially if we crave intimacy and connection? We all need other people. For seventy-five years, Harvard has been studying Adult Development, and looking at the ingredients of a happy life. They found that meaningful relationships are the key.

No matter what the origin of our social anxiety is, we need to build or rebuild social trust. The only way to do that is to be around safe people. This is a delicate, ongoing balance of safety, healing, and risking social engagement. As we heal, we are less reactive. We feel safer, and from this base we can move out into the world and experience new social situations.

Can you overcome your fear and do this? Yes! In conjunction with deeper healing, you can use simple strategies like exhaling six seconds to activate your body's relaxation response. Put your focus on someone else. Remember a few conversation starters. A healthy sense of alertness is necessary but not too much. We can learn to trust wisely as we engage with others.

Read over your list before you leave.

Practice breathing and relaxation at home on a regular basis and just before you leave.

On the way, focus on your breath, long slow exhalations of six seconds.

At the event, speak some of the time in longer sentences of at least six seconds.

Relax your forehead and let go of worry and anxiety. Soften your jaw and shoulders.

Look for someone who seems nervous to be there. We are never the only one with social anxiety. Go over with a smile.

Conversation starters: Where are you from? What do you do for work? What do you do for fun? How do you know our hosts?

Keep coming back to breathing, relaxing, and longer exhalations.

Plan for some extra rest and relaxation after the event. Putting ourselves out there and taking social risks is taxing for our nervous system. It is helpful to allocate time before and after the event to nurture ourselves and rest.

Coping with Physical Pain

Chronic pain can range from mild to severe, from an aching back to sharp, fiery pain in the head. It is exhausting and debilitating. No one wants to experience pain, whether it be emotional or physical.

Our brain and nervous system use pain as a warning. Pain can trigger feelings of threat or danger. This activates our fight/flight/ freeze survival system which creates a cascade of hormones, symptoms, and contraction that makes us feel worse.

It is a fairy tale that we are entitled to a life of ease, good health, and not too much loss yet we can feel cheated if our life doesn't work out the way we have envisioned. It is distressing to let in the suffering in the world and hard to accept it in our own lives. We may turn against ourselves, blaming ourselves for our health challenges and for not living up to impossible standards.

It is true that our minds and emotions affect our health. Lifestyle, stress, nutrition, and many factors influence our health. We all agree healthier actions improve our situation, yet it is difficult to go out for a walk or cook a nutritious meal when we're exhausted or in pain. Kindness and compassion need to be a foundation for inquiry, for taking responsibility, for accepting the reality of our situation, and for letting go of judging.

It is interesting to see our stories operating around pain. There can be a sense of "why me?" or a feeling that we are being punished. "What-ifs" are common. There is very often a fear that the pain will never end. We will never feel better and never recover.

Catastrophic, anxious thoughts sweep through and carry us further into suffering. We instinctively tighten and contract against pain. Resistance makes it worse.

Mindfulness, calming breath, meditation, relaxation, good sleep habits, and methods like the Living Inquiries and Natural Rest can help support our nervous systems while we recover and deal with chronic pain. Working skillfully with thoughts allows us to observe them for what they are – words and images arising in the mind paired with sensation in our body.

Having said that, even short-term pain in our body is intensely challenging for most people. Long term chronic pain and illness can take all of our energy and attention. It is an advanced practice to remain mindful as we deal with physical pain.

Kindness, compassion, and patience help. Ongoing pain in our body is not something anyone deals with perfectly.

Social Media and the News

Fear sells. It works on our human biological need to be alert to possible danger to keep us safe. People, politicians, and corporations deliberately manipulate us by using our survival system responses against us.

This is why disasters and danger dominate the media. As we become numb with repeated exposure, they make the images gorier and the rhetoric more terrifying.

It is not possible to have a healthy nervous system when we are exposed to this level of violence and fear several times a day.

I opted out of mainstream media in the late 1980s when I was working for several years with an AIDS organization. Watching television news and reading newspapers were simply too disturbing and draining given the intensity of my work. I consider myself well enough informed and I am engaged with society. By limiting the access of fear-based media, I don't have to work as hard to repair the damage to

112

my nervous system from daily exposure to the "news".

Feeling Angry and Powerless

Do you feel despair, anger, and frustration along with a sense of futility when faced with the suffering in the world?

> **"To be black and conscious in America is to live in a constant state of rage."**
> **James Baldwin**

Living in a constant state of rage takes a tremendous toll on our nervous system. So does trying to push it out of awareness. What are some healthy ways of staying awake **and** taking care of ourselves?

First, reduce your contribution to collective anxiety and fear. Be mindful of how you participate in conversations and social media. Notice when your conversations are agitating and stirring up fear.

Bring yourself back to kindness and truth, awareness and compassion. This not the first time you have felt powerless and it can trigger old feelings. This is part of what gives current situations the power to take over. Inquiry helps release the Velcro from prior experiences. You will still have all the feelings about your present situation but you won't be hijacked by unresolved feelings of powerlessness from your past.

See if you can let go of words and images for a few minutes and feel sensation in your body. Breathe and relax as you acknowledge and are present with the feelings in your body. These are nervous system responses related to fight/flight/ freeze.

Redirect your energy into mindful action. What is a reasoned response? What could truly help? How can you organize with other people to reduce the threat and help everyone to move out of freeze into action?

Balance outward action and support for yourself. You are not at the mercy of your thoughts. You can disengage from fear- mongering media. Reduce your exposure and therefore the intensity of the impact to your nervous system.

Gathering Data to Figure It Out

Scientists look objectively at the evidence, gather data, and then come to a conclusion. People like to think we are objective. In fact, many of us have formed a conclusion first then look for data to back it up. Social media develops algorithms to show us content that reinforces our current beliefs. Our mind does something similar.

When a real-life situation arises that is agitating, many people are glued to the TV and social media with an intense compulsion to keep checking, to gather more data in an attempt to understand. There is a sense that, with enough information, we could figure out what went wrong. We could do something to protect ourselves or at least minimize the damage.

Being caught up in a compulsive, reactive thought pattern actually makes us less safe. Our fear is amplified by a focus on catastrophic thoughts, especially when they are reinforced by others and in the media. We are absorbed in disastrous what-if outcomes and compulsive data gathering in lieu of taking effective action.

Underlying these compulsions is the hope we would not feel as powerless if we knew more. It would be lovely if it worked that way. That is not how real life works.

"The greatest gift you can give
the world is a peaceful mind."
Swami Veda Bharati

I Don't Want It To Be This Way!

We have so many ideas about how things **should** be. Everyone experiences some resistance to "what is".

It's Not Fair!

All through my childhood my mom said "Whoever told you life would be fair? It's not!" I likely responded "It should be!" I later put that to use as an activist for social change but these "shoulds" are sticky for many of us. Consider the following.

Janice works hard but was passed over for a promotion in favor of a guy who spends his time currying favour with the boss. She seethes inside when her colleague brags about the new boat he bought with the raise.

* * *

In the late 1980s, most people who contracted HIV went on to develop AIDS and die within a few years. Young gay men faced the sudden loss of their lives as they knew them, death of friends, coming out to their families, and social shunning. It was an intense process and nothing about it felt fair. It was hard to accept this reality.

Inquiring into these situations can be rich because of all the other times in our lives we felt powerless when something was unfair. There will likely be many memories coming up and sensation or feelings about them. Sometimes we can have an impact on the external situation. Often we can't. The only leverage we have is to work with letting it go ourselves.

The Living Inquiries are a great tool. We can inquire to see "what does this mean about me?" We might use the Anxiety Inquiry to look for what exactly it is that upsets us so much. As we see the connections, they lose their power.

Negative Judgments and Shaming

Many people believe we must push and shame ourselves to get anything done. "Get with it, lazy." In fact, pushing and shaming are not just ineffective but actually impede us. We may rebel against our own "you have to" orders or feel ashamed and not tackle our work with our full creativity.

Let's use the example of body shaming, which is prevalent in our culture, internalized, and so powerful. People act on their mistaken belief that making people feel ashamed of their weight or eating habits motivates them to lose weight. Fat shaming makes us feel terrible about ourselves and directly leads to disordered eating and more weight gain.

Shaming makes it harder to change

Most young children experience judging and harsh words from their peers or caregivers. After a time we may "take over the job" and do it internally to ourselves as well. It happens when a woman makes critical remarks about her own body and a young woman hears her and internalizes it. It happens every day with images in popular culture and media.

People can feel quite entitled to judge and shun us. It hurts. We respond in a variety of ways in the moment. The most important thing is to apply kindness and not jump on the train of denigrating and ridiculing ourselves. We can stop adding to our own suffering.

Would you want to be friends with someone who talks to you the way you often talk to yourself? This is a habit and pattern of stress response that we can attend to and change with attention and compassion. We can apply this to a variety of unkind thoughts about ourselves.

Our Inner Voice and Reframing

Have you ever noticed thoughts like the ones on the next few pages running through your own mind? Look through the examples and see where you might be willing to lighten up and give yourself a break.

After I had been meditating for about a year, I made a mistake and called myself stupid. It stopped me in my tracks because I realized it was the first thought like that I had experienced in many months. Those negative judgments had mostly fallen away. I can tell you that recognition really inspired me to continue to meditate.

Have you ever heard some of these thoughts in your own mind? If so, try reframing what you are saying to yourself. That alone helps tremendously in becoming friends with ourselves.

I'm an idiot!

Wow, that is harsh. I could reframe that to the facts: I forgot to return her call.

I'm trying to meditate and I've been lost in thought for the last 10 minutes!

Bring your attention back now you've noticed. It's okay. It's the nature of the mind to wander.

When I was a child, I felt absolutely on my own.

That's scary, especially for a kid. Now I have my own back. I'm not alone anymore.

I'll never get better. I can't live with my brain always freaking out and with being so jumpy.

(Hand on my heart) It's hard being hyper- vigilant. This is normal with trauma. I can heal.

This plane could crash on take-off. We'll all die in a fireball. What if I have a panic attack and everyone will know I'm a loser?

I'll put my hand on my stomach to relax and focus on deep continuous breaths to calm myself down. That's better. I'm not a loser. I'm afraid.

My stomach is disgusting. I'm so fat. No one will ever want to be with me. I'll be alone forever.

I notice how much I suffer when I judge myself. I am not disgusting. (Putting my hand on my heart). I am here for you. I love you.

My daughter is an addict. I really screwed her up. I'm terrified she's going to die. I'm a terrible mother.

I wasn't strong enough then to see and take steps to protect my daughter when she was a child. I deeply regret that.

I'll never be able to make it on my own. I won't have enough money. I'll be too lonely. I was stupid about money when I was younger and now I'm going to pay for it. I should have ... I shouldn't have ... I was lazy and deserve to be poor. (Accompanied by gut-wrenching intense fear in the body)

(Hand on heart) It's natural to be scared of getting older, with or without sufficient money. Breathe deeply. Relax. I understand the bigger picture of how traumatized I was. I did the best I could then. I can at least be kind to myself now and do something to help me to feel safer.

Avoidance Strategies

When we practice mindfulness, we begin to know ourselves intimately. This is exciting, deeply satisfying, and completely scary.

This is simply part of our fight/flight/freeze survival system. When we are afraid and unable to get away from danger or abuse, we find a way to leave. If we cannot run away and escape physically, we may dissociate and escape emotionally. Trauma is then stored in our body as fear and other strong emotion. This affects us until we are able to process it later.

Intense or painful sensations can feel too threatening and we avoid them when we can. We may distract ourselves with something relatively benign like shopping, overwork, or screen time. Much of what is discussed in this book including anxiety, compulsive and catastrophic thinking, vary in level from mildly troubling to having profound negative effects in our daily lives.

Addiction is a desperate attempt to avoid feeling pain. When our pain reaches a level we can't handle, we find a way to manage it.

We can see that in the distraction-to- addiction continuum. Some people watch Netflix and have a few extra cookies or a drink after work to relax and self-soothe when they've had a tough day. For others, the compulsion to escape feels more like a freight train that drags them into hours of binge eating or drinking until they pass out.

We can heal and recover from these patterns and habits of our nervous system and mind.

Addiction

Addictions can be used in a mild form to "take the edge off" emotional or physical pain or to a degree all of us would recognize as addiction. Substances that make us forget or alter our perception of reality are ideal for escaping painful experiences. These include food, alcohol, and other drugs. Process addictions range from mild to severe and include gambling, sex, over-work, gossip, and shopping.

We live in a culture built around avoiding and distracting ourselves from pain. We have socially approved process addictions like shopping and overwork, yet we shame people who engage in gambling, sex and porn, or substance addictions like alcohol and other drugs.

> *"Natural Rest is a simple revolutionary way to recover from addiction."*
> *Scott Kiloby*

The Kiloby Center for Recovery near Palm Springs California is the first U.S. addiction treatment center focusing primarily on mindfulness. The results are impressive. The Center addresses the trauma that underlies addiction through a holistic, comprehensive program.

Myself and licensed clinical psychologist Dr. Kay Vogt co-lead the Kiloby Center for Recovery program to support families. It is open to the public to anyone who has a loved one or family member with an addiction, whether or not that person is in recovery.

Healing our own patterns, anxiety, and fear is necessary for us to stop enabling addiction and to support recovery.

I highly recommend Scott Kiloby's book, DVD and program Natural Rest for Addiction.

http://naturalrestforaddiction.com/

Planning and Control

We try to plan for every eventuality in an attempt to feel safer. A minimal amount of planning is helpful. For example: *If I run into that person and I feel overwhelmed, I will remember I can get in my car and leave.*

We are not helping ourselves when we get too far into the loop of what-ifs, or when we make contingency plans for every situation we can imagine. What we visualize in detail is experienced by the nervous system and body. We don't need to add that additional fear.

Notice and acknowledge when this behavior is happening. Tell yourself: *I recognize there is fear and anxiety here. I am trying to soothe and comfort myself by controlling the situation.*

Many people feel helpless to work with thoughts in their mind. We don't actually have to follow along with whatever comes in. Learn to recognize the signs of when an unhelpful pattern of thinking has shown up, take a few deep breaths, and refocus your mind.

Perfectionism

Wanting things to be perfect is another way we try to calm ourselves down. Like obsessive planning, it backfires and creates more stress.

The deficiency story "I'm not good enough" can underlie this strategy. Wanting a person to be perfect is not realistic. Whether we put that pressure on ourselves or someone else, it leaves us feeling anxious and unsatisfied.

I didn't realize how much this was at play in my life until I started working with letting go of judgment. I discovered I had a lot of "shoulds".

I began to ask "Who wrote the rule that I must ...?" or "How do I know I should ...?"

Once again, kindness and compassion can transform the situation. I also remind myself that I don't get a gold star for pushing myself or trying to do something perfectly. It's not grade school. I don't have to placate someone. The world doesn't come to an end when I relax and go for a walk at the beach instead of whatever I think I "should" be doing.

Codependence

Codependence is outside the scope of this book except to say it can be another form of avoidance of our own feelings and taking responsibility for our own lives.

Another way to describe this is under- and over-functioning and is common around addiction. An adult child with drug addiction loses their job because they've missed so much work. The parents over-function by contributing towards rent, phone, and car payments, thus enabling the person to keep using.

Fear and anxiety underlie our dysfunctional patterns in relationships. Calming our own anxiety is how we can improve boundaries and work with our relationships.

**"We rescue people from responsibilities.
Then we feel used and sorry for ourselves. That is
the pattern, the triangle."
Melody Beattie**

Denial

A regular practice of allowing things to be as they are makes us steadier and better able to weather life's storms. The truth is we can't control what happens in life. That feels scary.

At a teacher training retreat in 2001, my meditation teacher gathered his teachers together to help us prepare for a meeting the following day. One of the senior teachers was angry and threatening to leave.

We were advised to go back to our rooms and let go of our previous relationship to her. He held up two closed fists. "This is what it is to hold onto what you had with her." He opened his hands. "Your old relationship is gone. Accept that. There is no chance of you being open to a new relationship until you let the old one go."

This teacher was very important to me and it was hard to accept she was choosing to leave our close-knit group in such a manner. I felt devastated for months and railed against the new reality. I finally had to let it go. It was not up to me.

133

Leaving the Scene

Dissociation is a clinical psychology term referring to detaching our attention from what is happening in reality. This can be mild or extreme, and is commonly experienced by people who have been abused and have Post Traumatic Stress Disorder (PTSD).

Children who are abused may report leaving their body when it was happening. They watched from above or blanked out altogether, not "returning" until the abuser was gone.

When working in the present with past traumatic events, dissociation can show up as numbing, confusion, sleepiness or a wandering mind.

Fantasy can be used as an escape when we are not able to physically change our situation. We can get quite detailed with our imagined scenarios. As with many coping mechanisms, it can be useful in moderation. Long term it could prevent us from taking appropriate action and it works against our ability to be present in the moment.

Lashing Out

Do you lash out when you are threatened? Lashing out can take the form of irritation, sharply critical or abusive words, "The Look", and intimidating body language. As we saw in the section about emotional flooding, when we feel we are in danger, we do whatever has worked in the past to protect ourselves. Our system does not care about our happiness, only to ensure our survival.

We all have a preferred strategy to avoid feeling helpless. Some of us direct our distress inward, and in that sense we don't threaten other people. Our "go-to" strategies or behavior depends in part on our personality and in part on our experience as children.

If we protected ourselves better by lashing out, that is what we did. If we put ourselves in greater danger by lashing out, then we tried to hold it in.

If you have this pattern of lashing out, it is essential to extend kindness and compassion to yourself first. It helps to learn about and understand why people lash out and hurt others. We develop these patterns for a reason. In some families we need a strong offense or we'll be eaten up. In others we need to stay off the radar to avoid being hurt.

Now is a perfect time to look and see how much you actually need to keep these strategies in play. It can feel effective because we are the one on top but actually there are high social costs to alienating people by acting this way.

Power over others is a potent antidote to feeling helpless. This survival level drive to avoid feeling powerless underlies emotional cruelty and bullying. Do you know that look of satisfaction on someone's face after they delivered a particularly devastating verbal attack and their victim is in pain? The internal experience of being on top is a compelling way to avoid feeling our own fear and insecurity.

Understandably, people whose pattern is to lash out have more interpersonal problems and amends to make after an outburst than people who turn inward, freeze, and numb when they feel threatened. As we heal, we can become safe for other people and experience the benefits of true connection and trust.

Even as we change, other people may be wary and stay away based on our past interactions. Their survival systems are trying to protect them. This is not personal although it is hard not to take it that way because the negative consequences of lashing out can be serious and long term.

We are generally unaware of our coping strategies and behaviors. These are driven by our survival system. With time and healing, the need for a fight response or for protection diminishes and opens up space for working with the damaging behaviors.

Kindness and compassion are the base or foundation for becoming friends with our mind.

"When we know better, we do better."
Dr. Maya Angelou

Righteous Indignation

This was a big one for me and one of the first clues I used in mindfulness practice. It often showed up as *"What kind of an idiot would ..."*. I could see the pattern was causing me suffering so when I noticed those words, I stopped and checked in to see what was going on inside.

Go for a drive as people jockey for position on crowded roads. This often triggers varying levels of intensity from irritation to road rage.

A co-worker doesn't share our work ethic and spends significant amounts of time updating her Facebook page and we do her work. We resent our co-worker and the boss who won't manage her.

This was interesting for me to watch in yoga class. I would notice a negative thought about the teacher, like "Why is she having us hold this pose so long?" When I tuned in, I saw I was struggling and would not give myself permission to come out of the pose ahead of the others. The teacher genuinely and often affirmed taking care of ourselves and modifying the pose so it worked for us. This was not coming from the teacher. Once I recognized the pattern, I used those thoughts as a clue to turn inward and work with allowing myself ease in my practice.

In the past, I was often caught in an escalating cycle of compulsive thinking and indignation. It feels satisfying to go on a rant and share our frustration with others who feel the same. It doesn't actually help.

We get so stirred up that it follows us home and we can't get it out of our minds. We may repeat it to others. We can't sleep. Around we go. Inquiry can help get to the root of what is bothering us. It could be triggering feelings of powerlessness from earlier in life.

Friends With Your Mind

As we near the end of this book, let's take a fresh look at your relationship with yourself. As you learn more about your system, your patterns and habits change. Suffering begins to release.

You understand more about how your system works. You can often recognize the mechanical nature of your thoughts and stimulus-response in your body and nervous system. You are able to step back, observe thoughts coming and going, and attend to the sensation itself.

**"You have to be with that pain,
but you have to have support."
Dr. Gabor Maté, MD**

You have tools to break down your experience into words, images, and sensations. Your responses and distress are no longer a mystery. Velcro is beginning to release as you use the inquiry and resting practices.

Many of us have no idea how much fear and anxiety operate as the background in our lives until we start to see and challenge our reflexive turning away and avoidance.

It takes courage and persistence to do this work. As we heal, we are no longer as hijacked and triggered by our past when we felt overwhelmed and powerless.

I can tell you from my personal experience that it is worth it. The result of this work is freedom. Space opens up to enjoy our lives. We are able to risk reaching out and connect authentically with other people.

"Gentleness is a sense of good heartedness towards ourselves. Precision is being able to see very clearly, not being afraid to see what's really there, just as a scientist is not afraid to look into the microscope."
Pema Chodron

Compassion

Compassion happens first within ourselves. Can we actually have compassion for others if we don't feel it for ourselves?

Here is an example from my own life. Several years ago a good friend was unable to leave an unhealthy relationship. Many of us know that place. We're stuck, knowing it is not good for us to stay but we are not able to leave.

We have our reasons for staying, including children, finances, social status, not wanting to admit failure, being afraid of loneliness, and fear of reprisal. We know and talk about how bad it is but can't leave. We would naturally have sympathy for a friend in that situation.

The problem was my underlying belief that she **should** leave. There was a sincere desire for her to not suffer. I didn't see it then but the truth is I also found it difficult to be a witness to her suffering. An obvious way to calm my own fear and anxiety would be for her to leave her relationship and start anew.

142

She picked up on my underlying anxiety. To her, it felt like I was judging her as not being good enough or not making the right decision. When I realized that, I took a big step back in my efforts to help.

I realized there was an arrogance in my idea she should handle her life differently. It was partly my own anxiety driving my wanting to help. I did a lot of inquiry into that. I looked into what came up around my own personal and work relationships. I too had stayed in unhealthy situations.

It was only as I understood and healed my own past that I was able to get it. It is not up to me to decide anything about someone else's life, or even to have an opinion about it. It is very easy to see what someone else "should do" or even what I "should do". So what? When it is used as a stick to make myself or someone else feel bad for not measuring up, it is not helpful and I need to let it go.

**I stopped wanting myself and
other people to be different.
The anxiety dissipated and
space opened up.**

Being kind is a practical way of working with ourselves. It means we recognize our humanity and that we stop heaping condemnation and self-loathing on top of our pain. It does not mean we sugar coat or deny the truth of what happened or that we approve of everything we and others have done. Having compassion does not absolve us or others from taking full responsibility for our actions. Forgiveness does not mean we condone anything. It means we work with letting go of wanting life to be different from what it is.

We observe what is happening internally within an atmosphere of kindness and compassion toward ourselves; just as we would with someone we loved, or someone who had helped us and cared for us. We can learn to understand being human and forgive ourselves.

"Once we are able to combine a feeling of empathy for others with a profound understanding of their suffering, we become able to generate genuine compassion for them."
Dalai Lama

Taking Care of Ourselves

What does self-care mean to you? Helpful options include increasing your focus on mindfulness, relaxation, meditation, and self-compassion practices. Care for yourself. Your nervous system is activated when you are scared and you need to actively down-regulate your system through rest.

Safety IS the treatment.

We cannot use reason to convince our nervous system to relax. We need to know, through our direct experience, in all the cells in our body, that we are safe. Only then will the energy related to fear or trauma dissolve on its own. Our definition of safe changes as our capacity and resilience improves.

I had two x-rays on my back over a 10 year period. I was convinced the pain between my shoulder blades must mean my spine was disintegrating. It felt real and very physical. Two years ago I had a breakthrough in healing my own trauma. I was shocked that my shoulders and back relaxed and the pain disappeared.

We can in fact learn to be present with the feelings in our own bodies when we have openness, stability, strength and support. The intensity decreases and it becomes just a sensation. We can see and observe it. This is what it feels like. It comes and goes.

Good self-care includes being selective about what you take in through social media and news outlets. The impact of much of the media these days is to scare people, not to inform us. They cleverly manipulate us through the negativity bias of the mind and nervous system.

We need to heal our own anxiety through good self-care as the foundation for a happy, fulfilled life and to how we engage in the world.

Healthy Mind

You have a mind that serves you. Imagine this in detail. Let yourself really feel it. You could also go to the page on our website and use these as affirmations.

I feel calmer, less anxious. There are fewer and less intense compulsive, catastrophic thoughts. When they come, I notice them as a clue to look deeper. I recognize unhealthy patterns. I am kind and firm with my mind.

I notice when I tense up or contract. I regularly practice breathing and relaxation. My nervous system has largely healed and overall I feel pretty resilient. I am confident I can handle life.

Things still bother me at times but they do not have the same grip they used to. I am familiar with the sensations in my body. They might be painful but they don't scare me. I am comfortable inquiring into what they mean. Over time, most of my painful memories have resolved themselves. They don't have the impact they used to.

When I am suffering, I am able to hold myself in compassion and I am better able to freely let go. I am patient and understanding with myself and my inner voice is kind.

I give myself space and time to listen to my intuition. I have stopped pushing and have let go of the aggression of always wanting to be better. I understand my system and how to make it work for me. I take good care of myself.

As I heal my own mind, I become more available both to myself and to other people. Creativity and vibrantly alive interest have returned along with the ability to enjoy my life. I know in every cell of my being that I am okay.

I am friends with my mind.

Guided Practices

http://FriendsWithYourMind.com/

Visit our website to learn more about the book, to participate in guided practices, and to sign up to work personally with Lynn Fraser.

You are very welcome to join us for a free half-hour live practice online every day.

Listen to recorded practices about the topics in this book including working with thoughts in the mind, calming anxiety, relaxing vigilance, and catastrophic thinking.

Some of the practices are two minutes to five minutes. Others are more leisurely and might last for twenty-five minutes. All can be accessed on my YouTube Channel.

We would love for you to join our community of people implementing the practices and strategies from the book.

Terms and Definitions

Mindfulness

Jon Kabat-Zinn defines mindfulness as "awareness that arises through paying attention, on purpose, in the present moment, non-judgmentally. It's about knowing what is on your mind."

Living Inquiries

Mindfulness self-inquiry that offers a specific method to slow down and look at thoughts and feelings. We look at three elements: words, pictures, and sensations. We ask one of three questions: Is that me? Is it a threat? Is there a compulsion or urge?

The Living Inquiries and Natural Rest, combined with twenty years of teaching meditation and yoga psychology, are the foundation of my healing work and this book.

Sensation, Energy, Feelings

These three terms are used interchangeably in the book and refer to an experience in our body, like butterflies in the stomach or apprehension felt in the back of our neck and shoulders. The emotion of sadness, for instance, will also be located in our body, perhaps as a feeling of heaviness in the heart area. Fear might be felt as a tight fist or clenching in the gut. This is our nervous system responding to our environment and experience. Charged energy or being triggered refers to a higher level of intensity. Unprocessed trauma is stored in our body as sensation or energy.

Deficiency Story

An (incorrect) core belief that forms with repeated exposure to experiences starting in early childhood. When we feel unloved, we begin to feel we are unlovable. When we are neglected, we feel we are unworthy of attention. We conclude that there must be something fundamentally wrong with us.

Velcro Effect

Words and images that are stuck to or associated with sensations, feelings, and energy in our body. We look separately at the three elements of words, images, and sensations to release the Velcro.

Natural Rest

An ongoing invitation to relax and notice there is a simple, restful awareness here in the present moment.

Scott Kiloby   Kiloby.com
Living Inquiries   LivingInquiries.com

Trauma

In this book, the term trauma is in reference to psychology, the brain, and the nervous system, not a physical wound. People often avoid facing trauma because it is so painful. We have already lived through the traumatic event or period but still feel the negative effects in our life. Respected trauma therapist Dr. Peter Levine refers to trauma as a dysregulation of the nervous system. It is possible to heal the nervous system and enjoy life after trauma.

Resource: The Body Keeps The Score, Dr Bessel van der Kolk

Adverse Childhood Experiences Score (ACES). Researchers at the US Centers for Disease Control (CDC) discovered in the 1990s that childhood neglect and trauma were far more pervasive than previously thought. Trauma has a lasting impact, negatively affecting all areas of people's lives including physical and mental health, finances, violence, and addiction.

Fight/Flight/Freeze Survival System refers to automatic processes generated in our primitive brain to ensure our physical survival. It activates when we perceive danger. People with trauma in their background are often stuck on yellow or red alert causing a multitude of problems.

Shock or Crisis Trauma refers to a terrifying event where a person experiences or witnesses a threat to their life or that of someone close to them. This can happen to a person at any age. First Responders and people in the military may experience this type of trauma in their work.

Chronic trauma refers to and includes neglect and abuse that occurs repeatedly over a long period of time. People experiencing chronic trauma may also have incidents of crisis or shock trauma where they feel their life is at risk.

Developmental or Childhood Trauma occurs when a child experiences or witnesses multiple exposures to abuse, abandonment or betrayal, and does not experience safe, consistent caretaking. The developing brain and nervous system are affected negatively. In addition, positive development fails to happen as it would if the child was safe and cared for. The effects of Developmental Trauma continue into adult life. People with Developmental Trauma who are highly affected in adult life may be diagnosed with Complex PTSD.

PTSD or PTS: Post Traumatic Stress (Disorder) develops in some people after a shocking, scary or dangerous event. This includes people in war and domestic situations. Symptoms include hyper-vigilance, flashbacks, nightmares, and severe anxiety. A background in childhood of Developmental Trauma can set the stage for acute PTSD later in life.

Post Traumatic Growth and Resilience

Most people recover from shock or crisis trauma within several months and some even experience Post Traumatic Growth and increased resilience. Dr. Martin Seligman is a pioneer in the emerging field of positive psychology that researches effective ways to increase our resilience and mental strength before and after traumatic events.

Resources

http://friendswithyourmind.com

Please go to our website to watch videos and find other helpful resources.